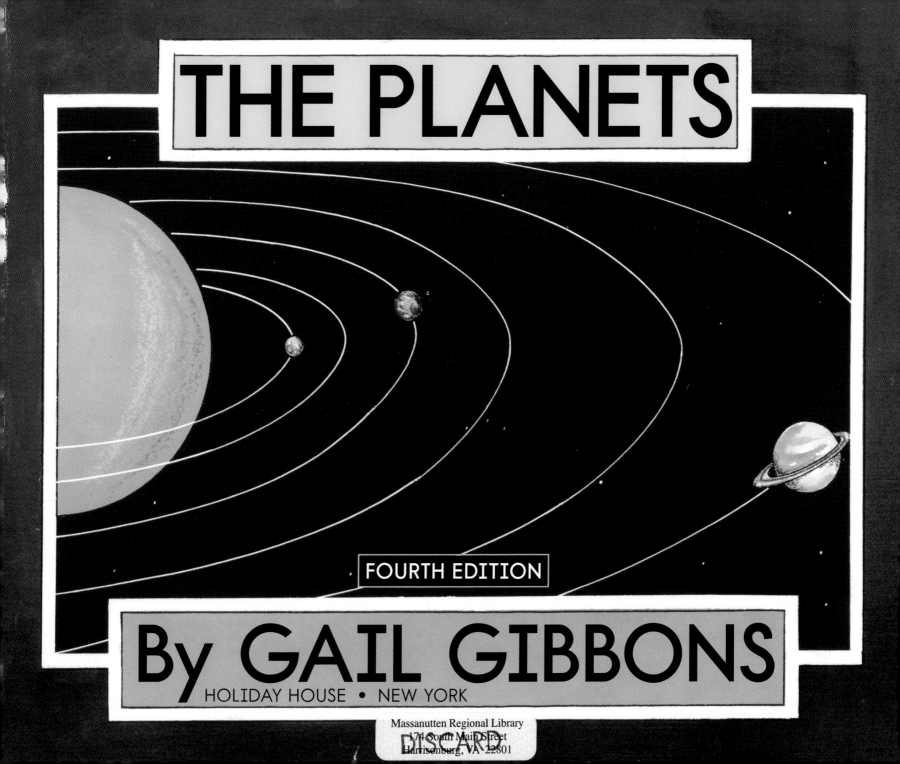

THE PLANETS

FOURTH EDITION

By GAIL GIBBONS

HOLIDAY HOUSE • NEW YORK

For Charlie Pratt

Special thanks to Professor Edward Foley, teacher of astronomy,
St. Michael's College, Colchester, Vermont; David Hogenboom,
Professor Emeritus of Astronomy, Lafayette College, Easton,
Pennsylvania; Dr. Andrew Schuerger, Mars astrobiologist,
University of Florida, and Zhuo Chen, Ph.D. candidate, Department of
Physics and Astronomy, University of Rochester

The Library of Congress has cataloged the prior edition as follows.

Gibbons, Gail.
The planets / by Gail Gibbons. — 3rd ed.
    p. cm.
 ISBN-13: 978-0-8234-2156-5 (hardcover)
 ISBN-13: 978-0-8234-2157-2 (pbk.)
 1. Planets—Juvenile literature. I. Title.
 QB602.G53 2008
 523.4—dc22
 2007033677

ISBN 978-0-8234-3966-9 (hardcover)
ISBN 978-0-8234-3967-6 (paperback)

PLANET

On a clear night when stars shine brightly, you might see what looks like another star. But each night it changes position in the star patterns. It is a planet. The word planet comes from the Greek word meaning "wanderer." All the planets except Earth are named after Greek and Roman gods and goddesses.

SUN

PLANET

STAR

A planet is different from a star. People can see a planet because the sun shines on it. A star shines because it is made up of burning gases that give off light and heat. Our sun is a star. Nearly every star is much bigger than the biggest planet.

In very early times, people knew of six planets. They were Mercury, Venus, Earth, Mars, Jupiter, and Saturn. Later, three more were discovered. They were called Uranus (YUR • uh • nuss), Neptune, and Pluto. Today there are eight planets in our solar system. In 2006, Pluto was designated a dwarf planet.

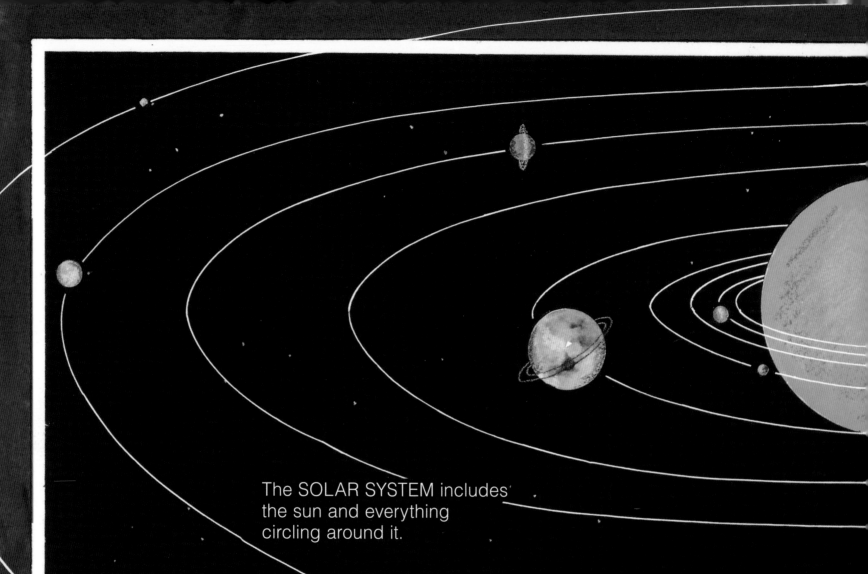

The SOLAR SYSTEM includes
the sun and everything
circling around it.

Planet Earth is where we live. It is one of the planets
that circle the sun. Together they make up the main
part of the solar system. The word *solar* means
"connected to the sun."

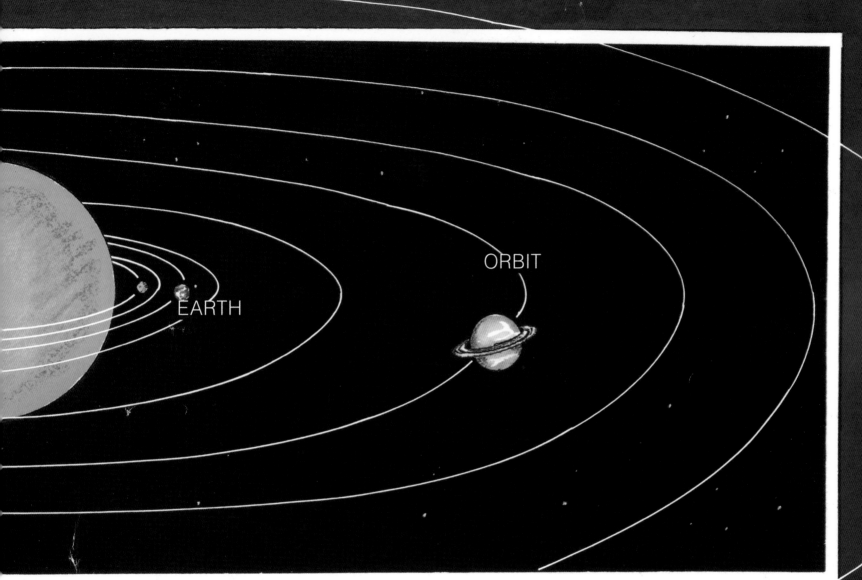

ORBIT

EARTH

The planets circle around the sun in paths called orbits.
The time it takes for a planet to travel around the sun is
its year. Each planet's year is different.

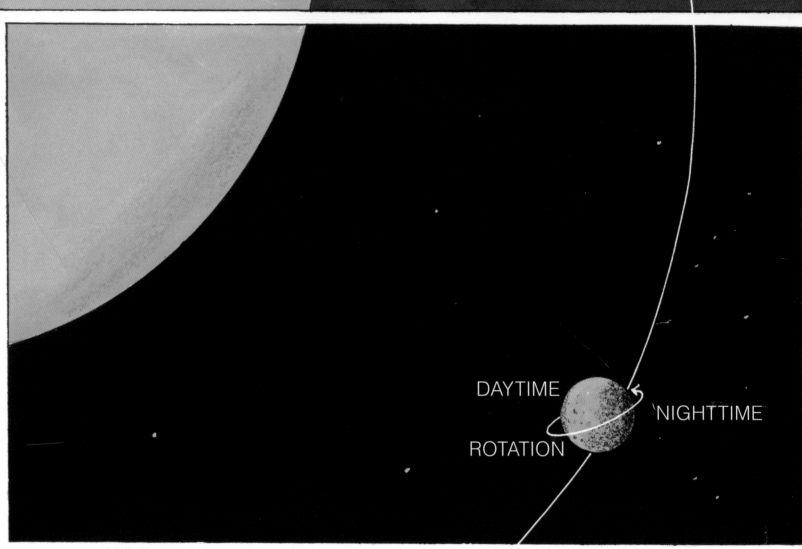

DAYTIME

NIGHTTIME

ROTATION

While a planet is orbiting around the sun, it is moving another way, too. It spins, or rotates. The time it takes for a planet to rotate is its day. Each planet's day is different. While a planet is rotating, part of it faces the sun. It is daytime there. On the other side it is nighttime.

TELESCOPE

People can look up on a clear night and might see Mercury, Venus, Mars, Jupiter, and Saturn. A planet looks like a steady point of light. A star twinkles. A telescope is needed to see Uranus, Neptune, and the dwarf planet Pluto, because they are very far away from planet Earth.

MERCURY

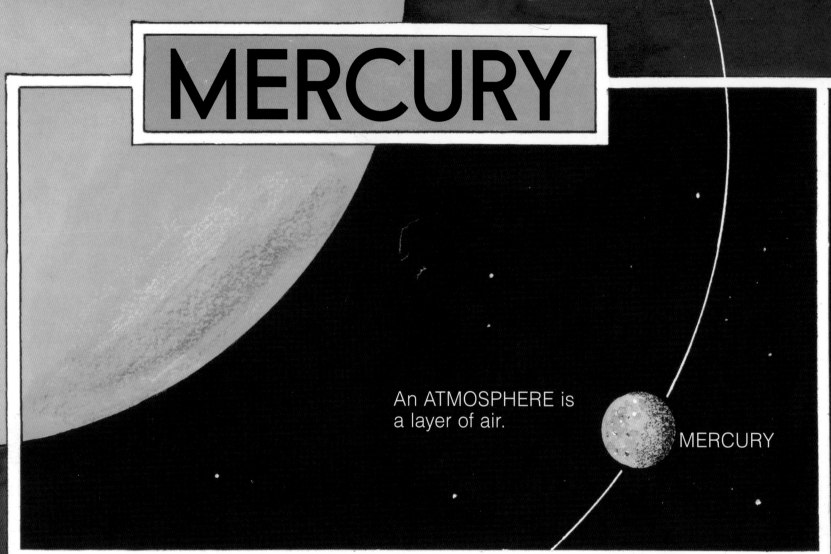

An ATMOSPHERE is
a layer of air.

MERCURY

Mercury is the planet closest to the sun. It is about 36
million miles (58 million km) away from the sun. During
the day it is extremely hot. During the night it is bitter
cold because Mercury doesn't have any atmosphere to
keep its heat from escaping.

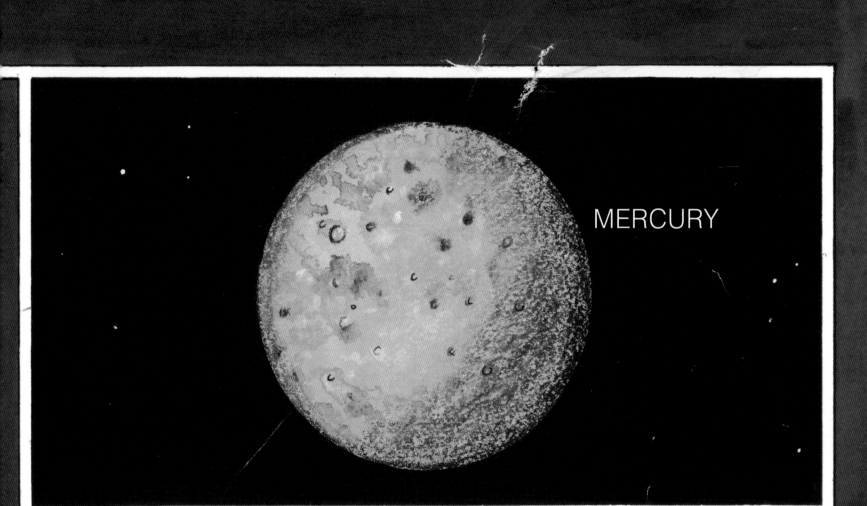

MERCURY

Mercury is the smallest planet in our solar system.
It is made up of rock and metal. One year on Mercury is
only 88 Earth days. That's how long it takes for
Mercury to orbit the sun. Mercury rotates very slowly,
so its days are very long. A day on Mercury is 59
Earth days.

VENUS

VENUS

Venus is the second planet from the sun. It is usually the brightest object in our sky, other than our sun and moon. At sunrise and sunset, it looks like a big, bright star. It is bright because Venus has a cloud cover that reflects the sunlight. These clouds are made up of gases.

MERCURY

VENUS

Venus is about 67 million miles (108 million km) away from the sun. It is hot there. Venus is almost the same size as planet Earth. One year on Venus is about 225 Earth days. A day on Venus is about 243 Earth days long because Venus rotates very slowly. On Venus, a day is longer than a year, and a year is shorter than a day.

EARTH

Earth is the third planet from the sun. It is the only planet known to have just the right environment for plants, animals, and people to live in. Earth is about 93 million miles (150 million km) from the sun.

A MOON orbits a planet. It has no light of its own. It reflects sunlight.

EARTH

VENUS

MERCURY

Planet Earth has just enough gravity to hold its atmosphere around it. Earth has one moon. Earth orbits the sun in about 365 days to make an Earth year. It rotates every 24 hours to make an Earth day.

MARS

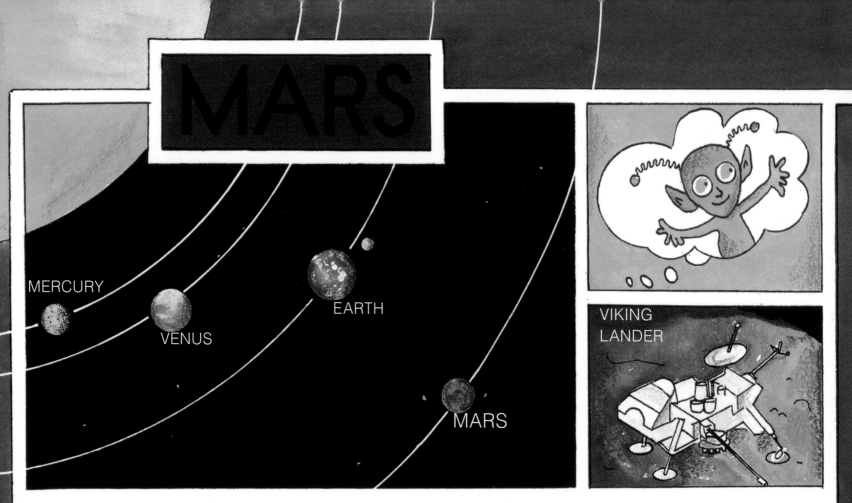

MERCURY

VENUS

EARTH

MARS

VIKING LANDER

Mars is the fourth planet from the sun, about 142 million miles (228 million km) away. People wonder if there was ever life on Mars. Although the surface of Mars is dry now, it once had rivers and perhaps even an ocean. In 2012, the Mars Science Laboratory's rover *Curiosity* landed on Mars to examine the planet's surface and climate. Scientists may still find evidence of life-forms.

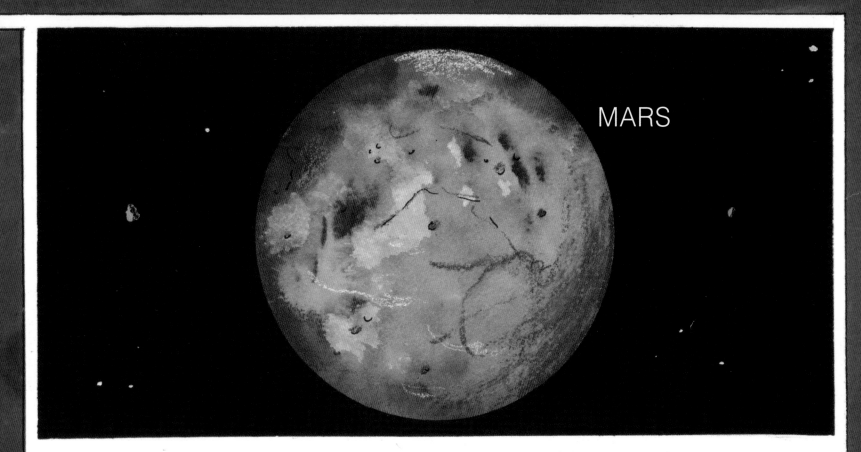

MARS

Astronomers believe that Mars looks red because iron on its surface has been rusted by the planet's thin atmosphere. It is very cold and is a little more than half the size of planet Earth. Mars has two small moons. One year on Mars is about 2 Earth years. A day on Mars is about as long as a day on Earth.

JUPITER

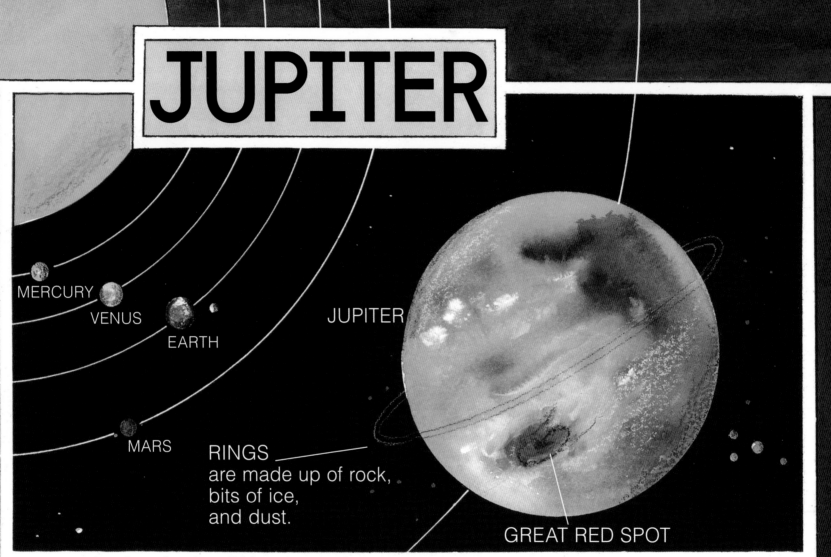

MERCURY

VENUS

EARTH

MARS

JUPITER

RINGS
are made up of rock,
bits of ice,
and dust.

GREAT RED SPOT

Jupiter is the fifth planet from the sun. It is about 484 million miles (778 million km) away. It is huge! It is bigger than all the other planets put together and has very thin rings around it. Jupiter is mostly made up of gases. Some of the gases form a giant red circle called the Great Red Spot.

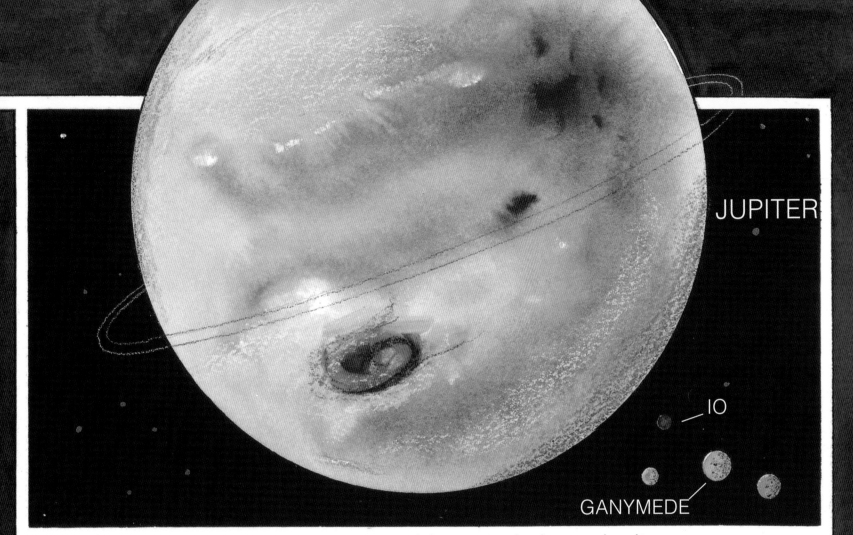

JUPITER

IO

GANYMEDE

At least sixty-two moons orbit around planet Jupiter.
One moon, Ganymede (GA • nee • meed), is the biggest
moon in the solar system. It is bigger than planet
Mercury. Another moon, called Io (EYE • oh), has many
active volcanoes. One Jupiter year is almost 12 Earth
years. It has short days, just under 10 Earth hours long.

SATURN

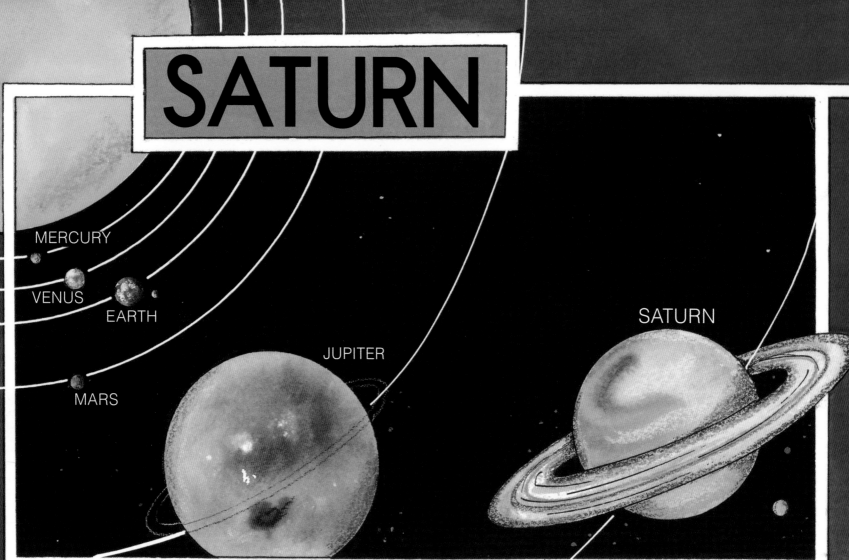

MERCURY

VENUS

EARTH

MARS

JUPITER

SATURN

Saturn is the sixth farthest planet from the sun, about 886 million
miles (1.4 billion km) away. It is the second largest planet.
Saturn's thousands of rings make it look different from the
other planets. The rings are made up of ice and rock. Some
pieces are as big as houses. On Saturn it is extremely cold.

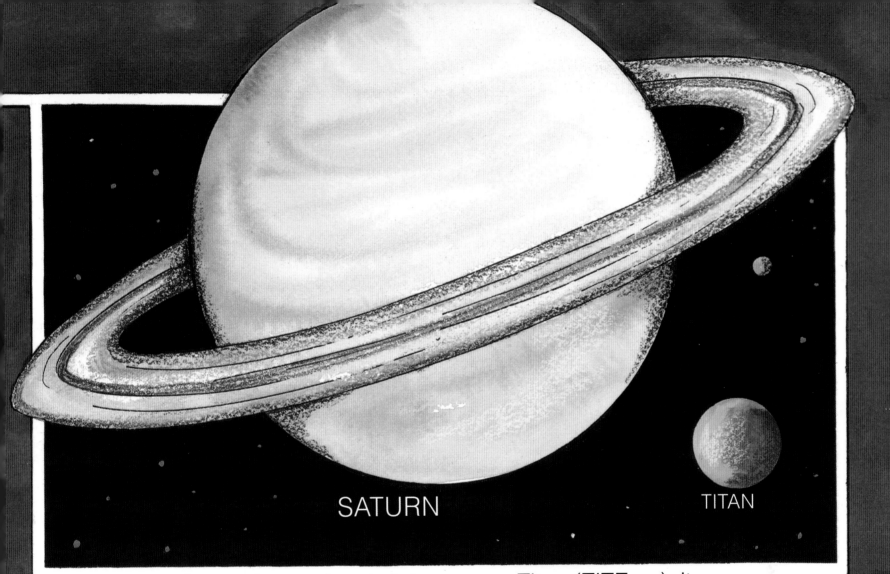

SATURN

TITAN

Saturn has at least sixty moons. Titan (TITE • n), its largest moon, is the only moon in the solar system with a dense atmosphere. It takes almost 30 Earth years for Saturn to orbit the sun. Saturn rotates in about 11 Earth hours.

URANUS

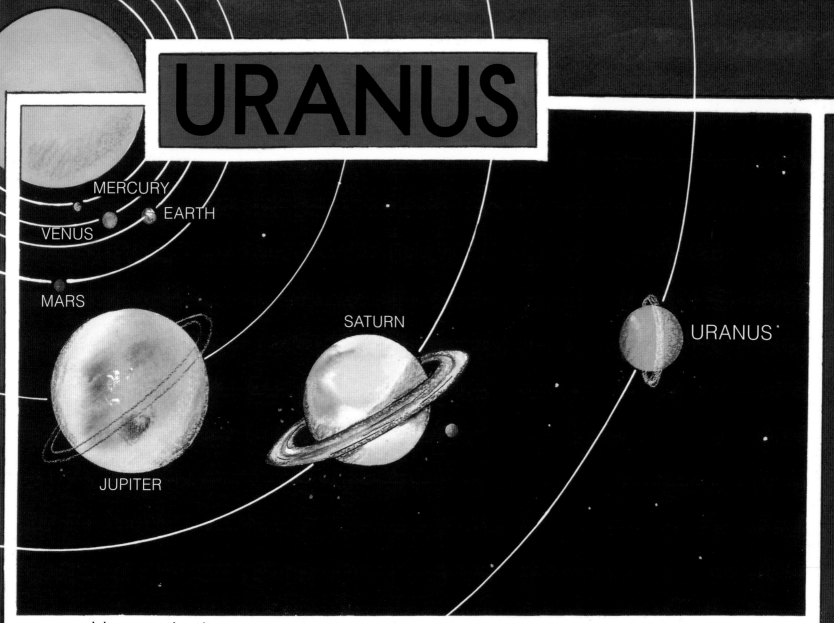

MERCURY

EARTH

VENUS

MARS

JUPITER

SATURN

URANUS

Uranus is the seventh planet from the sun. It is about 1.8 billion miles (2.9 billion km) away. It is so far away that from its surface the sun would look tiny. Uranus has eleven rings.

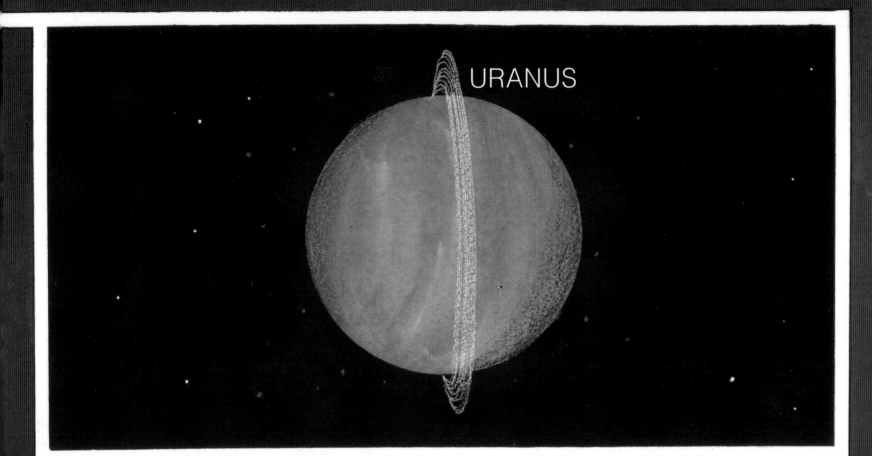

URANUS

Uranus is the third biggest planet, about one-third the size of planet Jupiter. At least twenty-seven moons orbit around it. Planets farther from the sun have longer orbits. They take more time to travel around the sun. For Uranus to make one orbit takes about 84 Earth years. Uranus rotates in about 17 Earth hours.

NEPTUNE

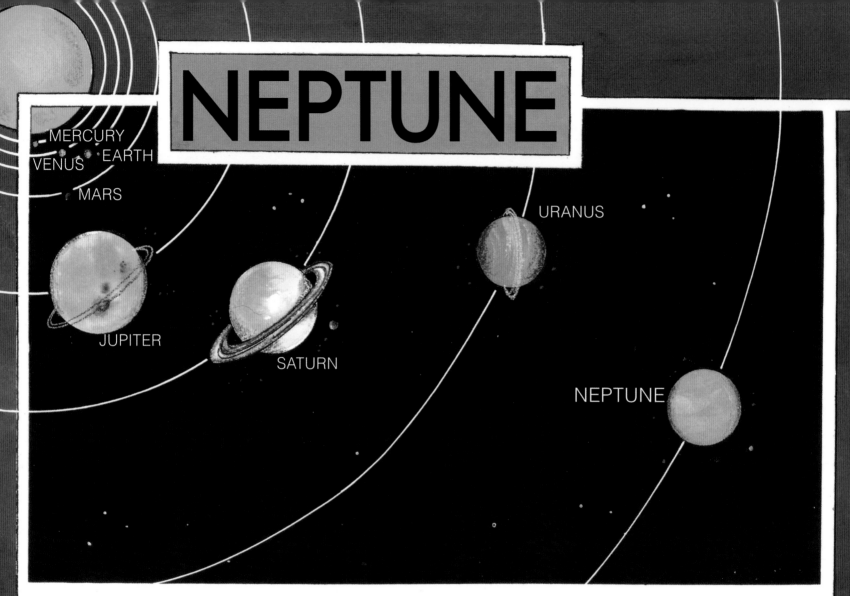

MERCURY
VENUS
EARTH
MARS
JUPITER
SATURN
URANUS
NEPTUNE

Neptune is the eighth farthest planet from the sun. It is about 2.8 billion miles (4.5 billion km) away. Neptune appears to be blue because of a gas called methane in its atmosphere. It is almost the same size as Uranus.

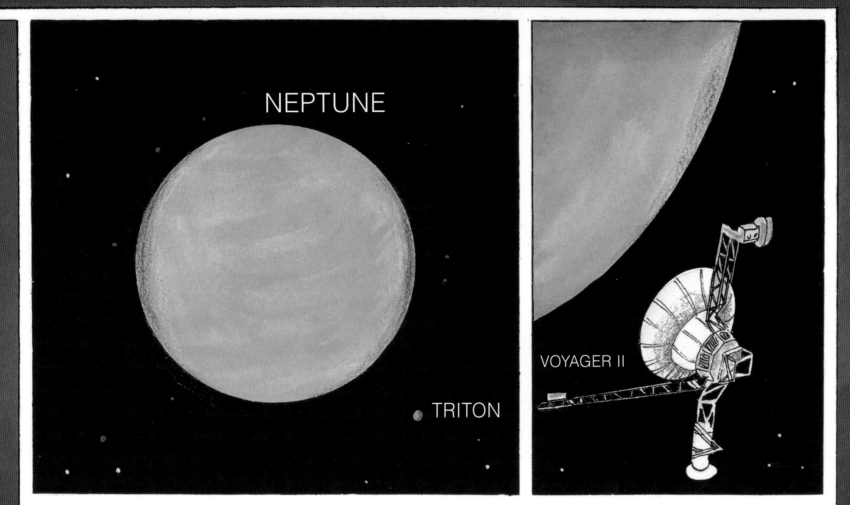

NEPTUNE

TRITON

VOYAGER II

One of Neptune's thirteen moons, Triton (TRITE • n), is about the same size as planet Earth's moon. The spacecraft *Voyager II* visited Neptune in 1989. One Neptune year is 165 Earth years. Neptune rotates in about 16 Earth hours.

PLUTO

MERCURY

VENUS

EARTH

MARS

JUPITER

SATURN

URANUS

After its discovery in 1930, Pluto was known as the ninth planet in our solar system. Now there are eight planets. Because of its size and unusual orbit, it has been classified as a dwarf planet. Sometimes its orbit carries it closer to the sun than Neptune. At its farthest, Pluto is about 4.6 billion miles (7.4 billion km) from the sun.

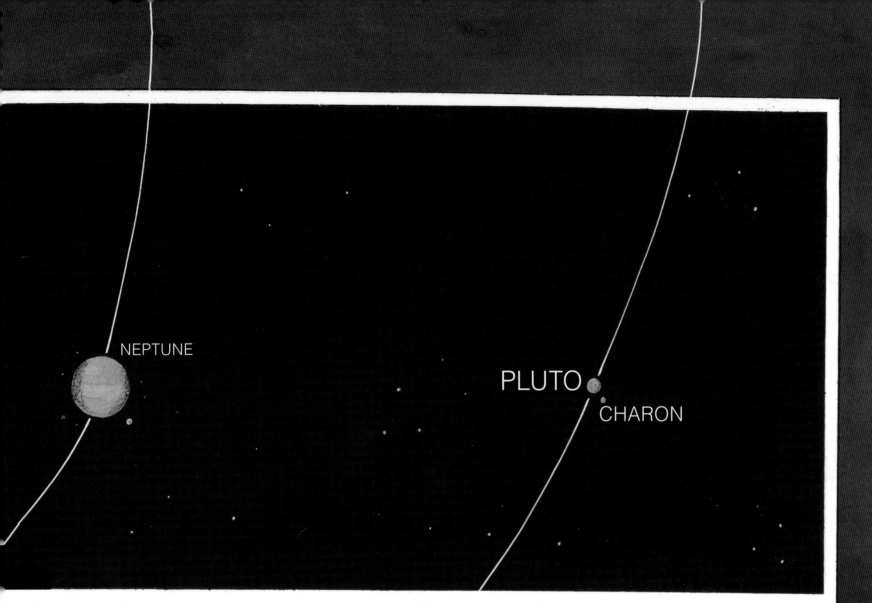

NEPTUNE

PLUTO

CHARON

Pluto is cold. It is smaller than Earth's moon. It has three known moons. The largest one is called Charon (KARE · un). One year on Pluto is about 248 Earth years long. A day on Pluto is about 6 Earth days long.

An ASTRONOMER is someone who studies the stars and planets.

Here on planet Earth, astronomers search the skies through telescopes. Spacecraft are sent into the solar system and beyond in search of new discoveries.

We are always learning about the planets, the stars, and what lies beyond. It is fun to search the night skies for planets and stars from our planet Earth.

MORE ABOUT OUR PLANETS

MERCURY

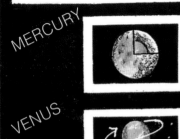

Mercury, which is bigger than Earth's moon, has a core of iron.

VENUS

Venus rotates in the opposite direction of the other planets.

EARTH

From outer space, Earth often looks blue because of its vast oceans, which cover more than half the planet.

MARS

Mars has a very large canyon. It is the biggest in the solar system. It is called Valles Marineris and is seven times longer than the Grand Canyon in the United States.

JUPITER

Jupiter is huge! If Jupiter were a big, empty ball, more than one thousand Earths would fill it.

SATURN

It is very windy on Saturn. Around its middle, winds blow at about 650 miles (1,000 km) per hour.

URANUS

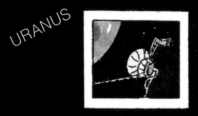

When the spacecraft *Voyager II* flew past Uranus in 1986, it had been traveling through space for nine years.

NEPTUNE

Neptune is thirty times Earth's distance from the sun. Some astronomers have said that studying Neptune from Earth is like studying a dime from a mile (1.6 km) away.

PLUTO

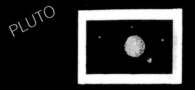

In 2015, the spacecraft *New Horizons* was the first to explore the dwarf planet Pluto and its moons.